Diet recommendations for TCM - Heart - Blood stagnation

Please check these recommendations always with a nutrition consultant, therapist, doctor or dietician. The recipes and the list of ingredients are supporting the conventional medical therapy.
The calorie disclosures of fresh ingredients (fruit and vegetables) vary according to quality and time of harvest. The contents were checked by a dietician and a nutrition consultant for the Traditional Chinese Medicine (TCM).

Author:
©2019 Josef Miligui
www.ebns.at

AF190357

Source:
The lists are created from the EBNS database for nutritional counseling. The database is used by dietitians, therapists and doctors for advising the patient / client.

Literature:
The specialist literature and the training documents of the German and Austrian dietary and traditional Chinese medicine serve as a knowledge base. We have used the documents as a basis of knowledge, adapted it to our experience and completed them.
http://di-book.com

Production and publishing:
BoD – Books on Demand, Norderstedt
ISBN: 9783746096810

Diet recommendations for TCM - Heart - Blood stagnation

1 Treatment strategy

Move blood, release stagnation, nourish blood and cool, calm mind - always over spleen and kidney!
Hot NO, cold NO, warm LITTLE (sweet YES salty NO), neutral refreshing YES.

2 Avoid

Bitter dehydrating food, very salty foods, hard to digest, too much acid (vinegar), pork, animal fats.

3 Breakfast

kkal. per serving

Baked chicory	230
Barley soup	265
Creamy potatoes with cauliflower	332
Millet with blackberries	348
Spinach flan with milk	250
Potato pancakes	893
Rice with parsnips	206
Tea from celery sticks	0
Tea from juniper berry	10

4   Snack

5   Lunch

6   Afternoon

7 Dinner

8 Any time

9 Recipes

(rec.) = You can use more.
(little) = You should use less than specified
(omit) = omit.

9.1 8 treasures of rice

Strengthens kidney and bladder, builds up Qi, strengthens the spleen, repels moisture, reduces internal heat, prevents cancer, builds heart, calms nerves.
Cooking time approx. 1 hour
Calories p. portion: 223
4 portions

Quantity of ingredients:
Lily bulbs 1 table spoon / 5g. () - cool - sweet, bitter .... *
Longane 1 table spoon / 5g. (rec.) - warm - sweet .... *
King Solomon's-seal 1 table spoon / 5g. () - neutral - sweet, bitter .... *
Yam root, yam root tuber 1 table spoon / 5g. (yes) - neutral - sweet............... *
Coix (seeds) YiYi Ren 1 table spoon / 5g. (yes) - cool - sweet, neutral............ *
Rice wild (nature rice) 1 1/2 cups / 240g. (yes) - neutral - sweet, bitter..... metal
Water 8-10 cups / 800g. (yes) - cool - salty..earth

Cooking instructions:
Each one 1 tbsp: Bai He, Longan, Yu Zhu, Da Zao, Shan Yao, Lian Mi, Yi Yi Ren, Qian Shi
Add hot water and soak for about 30 minutes. Then add 1 - 2 cups of rice (normal) and simmer for 1/2 to 1 hour until the rice is very soft. Or: Cook for about 3 hours with the herbs a congee. Then the herbs do not have to be soaked.

9.2 Baked chicory

Refreshing, brings the Qi down.
Cooking time approx. 20 min
Calories p. portion: 230
2 portions
Allergens: AG

Quantity of ingredients:
Chicory 4 pieces / 500g. (yes) - cool - sweet, bitter......................................fire
Cream, sweet 30% 2 table spoons / 40g. (yes) - neutral - sweet ....earth
Breadcrumbs (bread roll) 2 table spoons / 20g. (little) - cool - sweet, ... wood
Rice Basmati 1/2 cup / 60g. (yes) - neutral - sweet.................................. metal

Water 3 cups / 300g. (yes) - cool - salty ....earth
Salt 1 pinch / 1g. (little) - cold - salty ....water

Cooking instructions:
Blanch chicory in hot water whole for about 5 minutes; place in a
casserole dish; put some sweet cream over it; put the bread crumbs
over the chicory and gratinate.

Place the rice in salted water, heat till it boils and let it simmer over low
heat for about 15 minutes.

9.3   Barley soup

Works neutral to slightly warming and relaxes the Qi flow. Helps with
loss of appetite and diarrhea due to spleen weakness. With weak
spleen qi, one should often eat salty soups for breakfast.
Cooking time approx. 25 min
Calories p. portion: 265
2 portions
Allergens: A

Quantity of ingredients:
Barley 1 cup / 120g. (rec.) - cool - sweet, little salty ....earth
Salt 1 pinch / 1g. (little) - cold - salty ....water
Ginger fresh 1/2 teaspoon / 1g. (little) - warm - acrid ....metal
Olive oil 1 table spoon / 10g. (yes) - cool - sweet.......................................earth
Parsley 3 table spoons / 30g. (rec.) - warm - bitter.....................................wood
Water 1 1/2 cups / 240g. (yes) - cool - salty..earth

Cooking instructions:
Roast the barley in the pan, then grind it to the ground, and boil with
water, some salt and ginger to a mash. Before
serving add oil and parsley.

Variant: You can add a better taste to the dish if you cook it with
prepared vegetable or meat broth.

9.4   Basic recipe for a chicken broth worming

Strengthens Qi and blood, is very warm.
Cooking time approx. 2-3 hours
Calories p. portion: 90
9 portions
Allergens: L

Quantity of ingredients:

Chicken meat 1/2 piece / 600g. (yes) - warm - sweet .... wood
Carrot 2 pieces / 150g. (yes) - neutral - sweet ....earth
Leek 1 stick / 45g. (little) - warm - acrid.. metal
Celery root 1 piece / 500g. (yes) - cool - sweet..earth
Ginger fresh 2 slices / 2g. (little) - warm - acrid .... metal
Juniper berry 1 teaspoon / 3g. (little) - warm - sweet, acrid, bitter.................fire
Bay leaf 3 pieces / 2g. (little) - warm - acrid .... metal
Water 4 cup / 900g. (yes) - cool - salty..earth

Cooking instructions:

Remove chicken parts from fat. Place chicken pieces in a saucepan with hot water and heat till it boils briefly, skimming any resulting foam. Add coarsely chopped vegetables and all spices and cook over medium heat for 2 to 3 hours. Strain the finished soup. Throw away vegetables and bones.

Tip: If you want to use the meat as a soup insert, take out after 45 minutes and return only the bones in the soup.

Refrigerate for later use.

9.5   Basic recipe for a vegetable soup, nutritious

Strengthens spleen and lung, regulates Qi flow, builds up Qi, dries out, passes downwardly, strengthens stomach Qi.

Cooking time approx. 2-3 hours
Calories p. portion: 48
5 portions
Allergens: L

Quantity of ingredients:

Olive oil 1 table spoon / 4g. (yes) - cool - sweet..earth
Onion white 1 piece / 60g. (little) - warm - acrid .... metal
Carrot 3 pieces / 200g. (yes) - neutral - sweet ....earth
Parsnip 3/8 lbs - 6oz / 150g. (yes) - cool - bitter...fire
Celery root 1 cup / 100g. (yes) - cool - sweet...earth
Ginger fresh 1/2 teaspoon / 2g. (little) - warm - acrid .... metal
Lemon 1/2 piece / 25g. (omit) - cold - sour.. wood
Juniper berry 6 pieces / 6g. (little) - warm - sweet, acrid, bitter ....fire
Thyme dried 1 pinch / 1g. (omit) - warm - bitter... metal
Lovage 1 table spoon / 3g. (little) - warm - acrid, bitter .... metal
Bay leaf 2 leaves / 1g. (little) - warm - acrid .... metal
Salt 1 pinch / 1g. (little) - cold - salty .... water
Water 3 cups / 650g. (yes) - cool - salty...earth

Cooking instructions:
Cut the vegetables into cubes.
Heat oil in hot pot, fry shortly onions and vegetables.
Add cold water, then add ginger, bay leaf and lemon juice.
Season with juniper, thyme and lovage. Cover for 2 - 3 hours on a low heat and simmer.
The used vegetables should be thrown away.
The basic recipe serves as a soup base and to refine vegetables, legumes or cereals.
If you want to eat vegetable soup immediately, add the desired vegetables half an hour before.
Refrigerate for later use.

9.6   Casserole with white cabbage and apples

Nourishes juices, pulls together, strengthens spleen and liver, strengthens blood, triggers stagnation, leads off, antiparasitic.
Cooking time approx. 2 hours and more
Calories p. portion: 252
3 portions
Allergens: CGL

Quantity of ingredients:
White cabbage 1,1 lbs / 500g. (yes) - neutral - sweet ....earth
Onion white 2 pieces / 50g. (little) - warm - acrid ....metal
Rapeseed oil 1 table spoon / 10g. (yes) - neutral - sweet ....earth
Water 1 cup / 25g. (yes) - cool - salty..earth
Basic recipe for a vegetable soup (nutritious) 1 cup / 200g. (yes) - neutral - * . *
Salt 1 pinch / 1g. (little) - cold - salty ....water
Pepper (ground) 1 pinch / 0,5g. () - warm - acrid ....metal
Apple (sweet) 1 piece / 200g. (yes) - cool - sweet, sour..............................earth
Chicken egg 2 pieces / 120g. (rec.) - neutral - sweet ....earth
Cow's milk (1.5% fat) 5/8 oz / 180g. (yes) - neutral - sweet ....earth
Sour cream 15% fat 4 table spoons / 50g. (yes) - cool - sour....................wood

Cooking instructions:
Preheat the oven to 180 ° C (circulating air: 160 ° C). Clean white cabbage, quarter and remove the stalk. Cut the herb into fine strips. Peel onions, halve and cut into thin rings. Heat oil in a tall pot and fry onion rings first and then roast the herb. Mix water with vegetable soup and pour on. Cook with the lid closed for about 15 minutes on a medium flame. Season with salt, pepper and cumin.
Wash apple, quarter, core. Cut into slices and place under the herb. Whisk eggs with milk, salt and pepper. Put the mixture in a casserole

dish and pour the egg milk over it. Bake in preheated tube, golden brown for 40 to 50 minutes. Smooth the sour cream. Portion the casserole on a plate and add a small amount of sour cream each time.

9.7   Chicken soup with egg yolk and parsley

Forces Qi and blood, is very warming, nourishes blood and liver, harmonizes liver and spleen, forces eyesight, preserves the fluids, contracts.
Cooking time approx. 10 min
Calories p. portion: 118
2 portions
Allergens: CL

Quantity of ingredients:
Basic recipe for a chicken soup (warming) 2 cup / 500g. (yes) - warm - *........ *
Chicken yolk 1 piece / 10g. (rec.) - neutral - sweet ....earth
Parsley 1 table spoon / 10g. (rec.) - warm - bitter .... wood

Cooking instructions:
Cook the chicken broth according to the basic recipe.
Heat broth and bubble the egg yolk. Sprinkle the chopped parsley over it and let it rest for about 2 minutes. Drink in small sips.

9.8   Chicken soup with green spelt, parsley and sake

Forces Qi and blood, is very warming, nourishes liver-blood, preserves the fluids, contracts, scatters and move Qi, moisturizes, reduces cold-evil, softens knots.
Cooking time approx. 1 1/2 hours
Calories p. portion: 150
2 portions
Allergens: AL

Quantity of ingredients:
Basic recipe for a chicken soup (warming) 2 cup / 500g. (yes) - warm - *........ *
Green spelt 4 table spoons / 30g. (little) - warm - sour.............................. wood
Parsley 2 table spoons / 14g. (rec.) - warm - bitter..................................... wood
Sake 1 dash / 2g. (little) - warm - sweet, bitter, acrid .... metal

Cooking instructions:
Cook the chicken broth according to the basic recipe. Add the ingredients in the soup and simmer 10 min.

9.9   Clear soup from goose

Forces spleen, stomach and lungs, relieves weakness, forces Qi, calms the stomach, gets Qi moving, directs upwards, strengthens spleen and liver, regulates Qi flow, moisturizes, relaxes, builds up Qi, spreads.
Cooking time approx. 2-3 hours
Calories p. portion: 334
6 portions

Quantity of ingredients:
Goose parts 1,1 lbs / 500g. (yes) - neutral - sweet.................................... metal
Carrot 1 piece / 100g. (yes) - neutral - sweet ....earth
Onion (shallot) 1 piece / 25g. (little) - warm - acrid, sweet........................ metal
Leek 1 piece / 250g. (little) - warm - acrid .... metal
Parsley 1 Twig / 4g. (rec.) - warm - bitter .... wood
Lovage 1 Twig / 4g. (little) - warm - acrid, bitter .... metal
Water 4 cup / 1000g. (yes) - cool - salty...earth
Salt 1 pinch / 0,5g. (little) - cold - salty .... water

Cooking instructions:
Simmer goose pieces with vegetables and herbs for 2-3 hours. Sift through a fine cloth and cool. Degrease and store in the refrigerator.

9.10 Creamy potatoes with cauliflower

Forces Qi, forces spleen, relieves inflammation, moisturizes, relaxes, builds up Qi, spreads, nourishes lung Yin, produces humors, cools inner heat, strengthens Qi and kidney Jing, harmonizes liver and spleen, forces eyesight.
Cooking time approx. 30 min
Calories p. portion: 332
1 portion
Allergens: CG

Quantity of ingredients:
Potato 3/8 lbs - 6oz / 150g. (yes) - neutral - sweet.......................................earth
Cauliflower 1/8 lbs - 2oz / 50g. (yes) - cool - sweet.....................................earth
Cow's milk (3.5% fat) 3 table spoons / 30g. (yes) - neutral - sweet............earth
Cream, sweet 30% 1 table spoon / 10g. (yes) - neutral - sweet ....earth
Butter organic 1 teaspoon / 10g. (yes) - neutral - sweet.............................earth
Parsley 1 teaspoon / 3g. (rec.) - warm - bitter .... wood
Chicken yolk 1 piece / 25g. (rec.) - neutral - sweet ....earth

Cooking instructions:
Wash the potatoes under running water, thoroughly wash the cauliflower in stagnant water.
Divide the cauliflower florets into small buds, cut the stems into pieces about 1 cm in size.
Peel the potatoes and cut into 2 cm cubes.
Heat the milk with the cream in a saucepan, add the potatoes and the cauliflower. Cook on low heat for about 15 minutes.
Put the vegetables in a plate, add the butter, the chopped parsley and the egg yolk and lightly knead and mix everything with a fork.

9.11 Millet with blackberries

Keeps fluids, moisturizes lungs, tonifies blood, cools blood, detoxifies, preserves the fluids, contracts, strengthens spleen and kidney, diuretic, strengthens middle heater, moisturizes.
Cooking time approx. 30 min
Calories p. portion: 348
2 portions
Allergens: H

Quantity of ingredients:
Water 1 1/2 cups / 240g. (yes) - cool - salty ....earth
Millet 1 cup / 100g. (rec.) - cool - sweet, salty ....earth
Walnuts 2 table spoons (grounded) / 18g. (yes) - warm - sweet ....earth
Linseed oil 1 table spoon / 10g. (yes) - neutral - sweet ....earth
Honey 2 table spoons / 20g. (omit) - cold - sweet ....earth
Ginger fresh 1/2 teaspoon (grated) / 1g. (little) - warm - acrid................... metal
Salt 1 pinch / 0,5g. (little) - cold - salty .... water
Blackberry´s 5/8 oz / 200g. (yes) - neutral - sweet, sour .... wood
Acerola fruit nectar or powder 1 teaspoon / 2g. (yes) - warm - sour.......... wood
Lemon Balm (fresh) 2-4 leaves / 1g. (omit) - cool - sour .... metal

Cooking instructions:
Simmer the millet for 5 min and let it swell for another 30 min.
Add the walnuts and cover the millet. Simmer on a low heat until soft.
Cook for 10-15 minutes. Season the millet with honey, fresh grated ginger, salt and acerola and leave to soak for another 10 minutes. In the meantime wash blackberries and finely chop lemon balm. Mix millet with blackberries and lemon balm and serve warm.

Tip: The millet can be well pre-cooked in the evening. In the morning just warm briefly, mix with blackberries and lemon balm and serve.

9.12 Spinach flan with milk

Forces Qi, forces spleen, relieves inflammation, moisturizes, relaxes, builds up Qi, spreads, forces blood, Yin and Jing, nourishes Yin, moisturizes in case of internal dryness, nourishes blood and Yi, forces Zang-organs.
Cooking time approx. 1 min
Calories p. portion: 250
1 portion
Allergens: ACG

Quantity of ingredients:
Potato 1/4 lbs - 4oz / 100g. (yes) - neutral - sweet......................................earth
Spinach 1/8 lbs - 2oz / 50g. (yes) - cool - sweet, rough ....earth
Chicken egg 1 piece / 65g. (rec.) - neutral - sweet......................................earth
Breadcrumbs (bread roll) 1 teaspoon / 3g. (little) - cool - sweet, salty....... wood
Cow's milk (3.5% fat) 6 table spoons / 50g. (yes) - neutral - sweet............earth
Crème fraiche cheese 1 teaspoon / 3g. (yes) - neutral - sweet..................earth
Butter organic 1 teaspoon / 3g. (yes) - neutral - sweet...............................earth

Cooking instructions:
Wash the potatoes and cook with a little water in about 20 minutes.
Heat the water till it boils. Clean the fresh spinach and add to the boiling water (the frozen unfreeze), bring to the boil again and boil for about 2 minutes. Drain the spinach and puree.
Peel the potatoes and squeeze them through the potato press or crush them with the potato masher.
Mix with the spinach, egg and breadcrumbs.
Grease a small, refractory form (about 300 ml) with the butter and pour in the vegetable musk. Put the dish in a saucepan and pour enough water into the saucepan that the dish is two-thirds in a water bath.
Cover and simmer for 15 minutes over medium heat.

Heat the milk with the creme fraiche.

Put the spinach flan on a plate and pour the milk over it.

9.13 Potato pancakes

Forces Qi, forces spleen, relieves inflammation, moisturizes, relaxes, builds up Qi, spreads, forces blood, Yin and Jing, nourishes Yin, Moisturizes in case of internal dryness, forces blood, forces spleen, calms nerves and stomach.
Cooking time approx. 15 min
Calories p. portion: 893
1 portion
Allergens: ACG

Quantity of ingredients:
Potato (mealy) 5/8 lbs - 8oz / 250g. (yes) - neutral - sweet ....earth
Wheat flour 1/2 oz / 10g. (yes) - cool - sweet, salty.................................... wood
Chicken egg 1 piece / 35g. (rec.) - neutral - sweet.....................................earth
Rapeseed oil 2 table spoons / 20g. (yes) - neutral - sweet.........................earth
Salt 1 pinch / 1g. (little) - cold - salty ....water
Cream sour 20% 1/8 lbs - 2oz / 50g. (yes) - neutral - sweet ....earth
Salt 1 pinch / 1g. (little) - cold - salty ....water

Cooking instructions:
Grater the peeled potatoes finely, add the remaining ingredients, mix well and salt. Heat the oil and add small flat cakes to the pan with the spoon. Roast the potato pancakes on both sides crispy golden brown. Place them on the plate with sour cream, salt and sprinkle with herbs.

9.14 Pumpkin slices with spicy rice

Forces lungs and spleen, diuretic, forces Qi, protects liver, warms the stomach and spleen, harmonizes the intestine, forces Qi, reduces moisture, directs upwards.
Cooking time approx. 45 min
Calories p. portion: 438
4 portions
Allergens: AG

Quantity of ingredients:
Clarified butter 1/2 teaspoon / 5g. (little) - neutral - sweet..........................earth
Saffron 1 Sachet / 0,1g. (rec.) - neutral - sweet...earth
Turmeric (yellow root) 1 teaspoon / 2g. (little) - warm - bitter ....*
Rice Basmati 1 cup / 120g. (yes) - neutral - sweet................................... metal
Water 1 cup / 120g. (yes) - cool - salty..earth
Salt 1/2 teaspoon / 2g. (little) - cold - salty ....water
Pumpkin 6-8 slices / 400g. (yes) - warm - sweet...earth
Barley flour 1 cup / 10g. (yes) - cool - sweet ....earth

Breadcrumbs (bread roll) 1 cup / 10g. (little) - cool - sweet, salty.............. wood
Salt 1/2 teaspoon / 2g. (little) - cold - salty .... water
Pepper (ground) 1 pinch / 1g. () - warm - acrid .... metal
Butter organic 1 table spoon / 10g. (yes) - neutral - sweet.......................... earth
Cream, sweet 30% 1 1/2 cup / 300g. (yes) - neutral - sweet....................... earth
Barley flour 2 table spoons / 20g. (yes) - cool - sweet................................ earth
Chives 3 table spoons / 20g. (little) - warm - acrid .... metal
Dill 3 table spoons / 20g. (little) - warm - acrid .... metal

Cooking instructions:

Melt the fat in a small saucepan, add saffron and turmeric, lightly roast
over medium heat for about 1-2 minutes to allow the aromas to develop
(note: the spices should never be burnt). Add the rice for about 2
minutes stir fry, add the salt, stir briefly and add the water, stir and close
the pot with a lid. Cook at low to medium heat until the water is almost
completely absorbed, then remove from the heat and set aside with the
lid still closed and let it swell. Do not stir! When the water is completely
absorbed, the rice is ready!

Mix flour, bread crumbs, salt and pepper. Moisten the pumpkin slices
with water or mashed egg, turn the slices in the flour mixture and fry
gently in butter until golden brown and the pumpkin is soft. Melt the
butter in a small saucepan, brown the barley flour in it and remove from
heat, add the sour cream, season with salt, pepper, add the chopped
herbs and pour the sauce over the fried pumpkin slices. Serve with the
rice.

9.15 Pumpkin soup

Forces lungs and spleen, diuretic, forces Qi, protects liver, forces Qi,
forces spleen, relieves inflammation, moisturizes, relaxes, builds up Qi,
spreads, strengthens spleen and liver, regulates Qi flow, moisturizes,
relaxes, builds up Qi, spreads.
Cooking time approx. 1 hour
Calories p. portion: 105
3 portions

Quantity of ingredients:

Pumpkin 3/4 lbs / 300g. (yes) - warm - sweet .... earth
Carrot 2 pieces / 100g. (yes) - neutral - sweet .... earth
Potato 2 pieces / 120g. (yes) - neutral - sweet... earth
Olive oil 1 table spoon / 10g. (yes) - cool - sweet...................................... earth
Onion white 1 piece / 50g. (little) - warm - acrid .... metal
Water 1 cup / 120g. (yes) - cool - salty... earth

Parsley 1 table spoon / 7g. (rec.) - warm - bitter .... wood
Anise (Common Fennel) 1 pinch / 1g. (little) - warm - acrid .... earth
Salt 1 pinch / 1g. (little) - cold - salty .... water

Cooking instructions:
Add the olive oil to the pan, add the diced pumpkin, diced carrots and potatoes. Roast them shortly, add the finely chopped onion, fill with water, add enough water to cover the vegetables at least 3 finger-widths. Boil at low heat.

Season with sea salt, add small cutted parsley, a pinch of anise (little). Allow to simmer for about 35 minutes. Then purée the soup and add some water, depending on the consistency of the soup.

9.16 Quick zucchini soup

Reduces mucus, preserves the fluids, cools liver fire, forces stomach Qi.
Cooking time approx. 10 min
Calories p. portion: 42
4 portions

Quantity of ingredients:
Zucchini 2-3 pieces / 500g. (yes) - cool - sweet .... earth
Onion white 1 piece / 50g. (little) - warm - acrid .... metal
Corn germ oil 2 table spoons / 6g. (yes) - neutral - sweet .... earth
Parsley 1 table spoon / 7g. (rec.) - warm - bitter .... wood
Chives 1 teaspoon / 3g. (little) - warm - acrid .... metal
Water 2 cup / 400g. (yes) - cool - salty .... earth

Cooking instructions:
Fry chopped onion in oil. Add sliced zucchini and sauté well. Pour with water. Chop parsley and chives, add and puree everything.

9.17 Rice with parsnips

Regulates Qi, dries out, passes downwardly, warms the stomach and spleen, harmonizes the intestine, forces Qi, reduces moisture.
moisturizes, relaxes, builds up Qi, spreads. distributes mucus, activates Wei Qi, forces Qi.
Cooking time approx. 45 min
Calories p. portion: 206
3 portions

Quantity of ingredients:
Rice variety any 1 cup / 120g. (little) - warm - sweet .... metal
Water 1 1/2 cups / 200g. (yes) - cool - salty .... earth
Salt 1 pinch / 1g. (little) - cold - salty .... water
Parsnip 3-4 pieces / 450g. (yes) - cool - bitter .... fire
Olive oil 1 table spoon / 10g. (yes) - cool - sweet .... earth
Sage 1 teaspoon / 3g. (yes) - cool - bitter, spicy .... fire

Cooking instructions:
Peel the parsnips and cut into slices. Fry for a short time in oil. Add the rice and fry again for a short time. Add the water and cook it at least 30 min. Sprinkle with fresh chopped sage.

9.18 Smoothie celery carrot (BIRRS)

Nourishes juices, strengthens spleen and liver, regulates qi flow, relaxes, builds up qi. Moves liver-qi, reduces cold-evil.
Cooking time approx. 10 Min.
Calories p. portion: 111
2 portions
Allergens: L

Quantity of ingredients:
Carrot 5/8 oz / 200g. (yes) - neutral - sweet .... earth
Celery sticks 1/4 lbs - 4oz / 100g. (rec.) - cool - sweet .... earth
Apple (sweet) 5/8 oz / 200g. (yes) - cool - sweet, sour .... earth
Basil (fresh) 2 table spoons / 5g. (little) - warm - acrid, bitter .... metal
Ginger fresh 1/8 oz / 5g. (little) - warm - acrid .... metal
Reishi mushroom 1 pinch / 1g. (yes) - cool - sweet .... earth
Salt 1 pinch / 1g. (little) - cold - salty .... water

Cooking instructions:
Wash and clean vegetables and divide into pieces. Puree all ingredients in a blender.

9.19 Spinach with Tahini

Nourishes blood and Yin, forces Zang-organs, forces stomach and intestines, harmonizes Qi, moisturizes lungs, forces Qi, forces spleen, relieves inflammation, moisturizes, relaxes, builds up Qi, spreads, nourishes blood.
Cooking time approx. 20 min
Calories p. portion: 150
4 portions
Allergens: N

Quantity of ingredients:
Potato 1,1 lbs / 500g. (yes) - neutral - sweet..earth
Salt 1 pinch / 0,2g. (little) - cold - salty ....water
Water 1 cup / 25g. (yes) - cool - salty..earth
Spinach 2,2 lbs / 800g. (yes) - cool - sweet, rough ....earth

Cooking instructions:
Cook potatoes and peel. Heat water. Blanch spinach. Shake off water and let it dry and stir with sesame.

9.20 Tea from celery sticks

Brings the Liver Qi in motion, cools heat, moisturizes, relaxes, builds up Qi, spreads.
Cooking time approx. 15 min
Calories p. portion: 1
4 portions
Allergens: L

Quantity of ingredients:
Celery sticks 2 table spoons (chopped) / 18g. (rec.) - cool - sweet ....earth
Water 2 cup / 500g. (yes) - cool - salty...earth

Cooking instructions:
Heat the water till it boils and put it aside. Add cutted celery and cook for 10 min. to let go. Strain. Sweet to taste with honey.

9.21 Tea from juniper berry

Dries out, passes downwardly, activates Wei Qi.
Cooking time approx. 10 min
Calories p. portion: 10
1 portion

Quantity of ingredients:
Juniper berry 1 teaspoon / 3g. (little) - warm - sweet, acrid, bitter.................fire
Water 1 cup / 125g. (yes) - cool - salty...earth

Cooking instructions:
A teaspoon of dried juniper berries for a cup of tea. Start cold and bring to the boil. Let it sit for 15 minutes, then strain.
This tea is unsweetened and swallowed, slowly drunk. The amount is enough for one day.

9.22 Tea from licorice (heart-strengthening)

Strengthen spleen and stomach Qi, nourishes Yin from heart and kidney, moisturizes, forces heart and kidney, reduces internal heat, preserves the fluids, contracts.
Cooking time approx. 15 min
Calories p. portion: 20
4 portions

Quantity of ingredients:
Dates red 2 table spoons (chopped) / 20g. (yes) - warm - sweet ....earth
Wheat 2 teaspoons (milled) / 16g. (yes) - cool - sweet .... wood
Water 2 cup / 500g. (yes) - cool - salty...earth

Cooking instructions:
Simmer licorice root, red dates and wheat for 40 minutes, strain and keep the tea in the refrigerator. Throw away the ingredients.
Variant: This recipe can be supplemented with chicken broth; it will be even stronger.
Decoction: 2-4 teaspoons, sprinkle licorice with 1/2 liter of cold water, heat till it boils, cook for 1 min, leave for 10 min. Drink 1 cup twice a day.

9.23 Tea from Longane

Forces spleen, builds up lung, builds up heart, calms nerves.
Cooking time approx. 10 min
Calories p. portion: 0
4 portions

Quantity of ingredients:
Longane 2 teaspoons / 4g. (rec.) - warm - sweet .... *
Water 2 cup / 500g. (yes) - cool - salty...earth

Cooking instructions:
Heat the water till it boils and put it aside. Add Longane and 10 min. to let go. Sweet to taste with honey. Strain when pouring.

9.24 Tea from red dates

Nourishes blood, promotes the build-up of Qi and blood, moisturizes lungs, produces humors, strengthens spleen and stomach.
Cooking time approx. 10 min
Calories p. portion: 12
4 portions
Allergens: O

Quantity of ingredients:
Dates dried 2-4 pieces / 15g. (yes) - warm - sweet ....earth
Water 2 cup / 500g. (yes) - cool - salty...earth

Cooking instructions:
Heat the water till it boils and put it aside. Add chopped dates and 10 min. to let go. Sweet to taste with honey. Strain when pouring.

9.25 Thick pea soup

Nourishes Qi, diuretic, harmonizes Qi (especially in the Middle and Lower), strengthens the kidney and the defense Qi, dischars moisture.
Cooking time approx. 2-3 hours
Calories p. portion: 123
3 portions
Allergens: AN

Quantity of ingredients:
Peas, green 3/8 lbs - 6oz / 150g. (rec.) - neutral - sweet ....water
Water 2 1/4 cups / 550g. (yes) - cool - salty...earth
Sesame oil 1 table spoon / 20g. (yes) - cool - sweet...................................earth
Onion white 1/2 piece / 25g. (little) - warm - acrid ....metal
Ginger fresh 1/2 teaspoon / 1g. (little) - warm - acrid ....metal
Ground 1/2 teaspoon / 1g. (little) - warm - acrid ....metal
Oat meal 1 table spoon / 15g. (yes) - warm - sweet....................................metal
Salt 1 pinch / 1g. (little) - cold - salty ....water
Parsley 1 stem / 2g. (rec.) - warm - bitter ....wood

Cooking instructions:
Soak dried peas before cooking. Sauté sesame oil, onion, a little oatmeal, ginger and cumin in a hot pot; add the peas and simmer for 2-3 hours; add salt at the end and purée with a blender; garnish with parsley.

9.26 Tsampa with jam or fruit compote

Nourishes fluids, reduces stomach heat, forces spleen, produces essence, harmonizes stomach, moisturizes intestines.
Cooking time approx. 5 min
Calories p. portion: 280
1 portion
Allergens: AGO

Quantity of ingredients:

Tsampa (roasted) 3 table spoons / 30g. (yes) - cold - sweet, little salty.....earth
Water 6-8 table spoons / 70g. (yes) - cool - salty ....earth
Butter organic 1/2 teaspoon / 2g. (yes) - neutral - sweet............................earth
Strawberry jam 1 table spoon / 7g. (yes) - neutral - sweet, sour .... wood
Sunflower seeds 2 teaspoons / 14g. (yes) - neutral - sweet........................earth
Apple (sweet) 1 piece grated / 120g. (yes) - cool - sweet, sour..................earth

Cooking instructions:

Pour Tsampa with boiling water and stir with a spoon until a porridge is formed.
Add butter, jam, sunflower seeds and grated apple.
Sweet to taste with honey, whole cane sugar, or barley malt.
Spices and herbs: fresh mint, vanilla or cocoa, anise, cinnamon

Summer: jam or compote of your choice
Winter: nuts and apple or pear

9.27 Vegetable porridge

Strengthens spleen and liver, regulates Qi flow, moisturizes, relaxes, builds up Qi, distributes, relieves inflammation, strengthens Qi, blood and Jing and middle heat, strengthens essence, preserves the fluids, pulls together.
Cooking time approx. 20 min
Calories p. portion: 161
1 portion
Allergens: G

Quantity of ingredients:

Potato 1 piece / 50g. (yes) - neutral - sweet..earth
Carrot (Early Carrot) 1/4 lbs - 4oz / 100g. (yes) - neutral - sweet...............earth
Chicken meat 1 oz / 30g. (yes) - warm - sweet .... wood
Butter organic 1 table spoon / 10g. (yes) - neutral - sweet..........................earth

Cooking instructions:
Wash the potato and put it unpeeled in a small pot. Cover with a little water and bring to boil, then cook the potatoes
on a low heat for 15-20 minutes.
Meanwhile, wash the carrots, clean, peel and cut into pieces about 2 cm in size. Steam with 3 tablespoons of water and the meat in a pot for about 15 minutes.
Finely chop the carrots and meat with a blender. Add the butter and puree everything.

9.28 Warming porridge

Forces Qi and defensive power.
Cooking time approx. 10 min
Calories p. portion: 357
1 portion
Allergens: AHO

Quantity of ingredients:
Oat flakes (whole grain) 6 table spoons / 60g. (yes) - warm - sweet.........metal
Fig dried 3 pieces / 15g. (yes) - warm - sweet...earth
Star anise 1 piece / 1g. (little) - hot - acrid...metal
Ginger fresh 1 pinch / 0,5g. (little) - warm - acrid ....metal
Water 1 cup / 120g. (yes) - cool - salty...earth
Maple syrup 1 table spoon / 10g. (yes) - cool - sweet................................earth
Walnuts 1 table spoon (chopped) / 8g. (yes) - warm - sweet ....earth

Cooking instructions:
Soak the dried fruit. Roast Oatmeal dry. Add dried ginger, star anise or cinnamon, a little grated ginger and boil everything with water to a mash. With maple syrup sweet. Whip grated walnuts and sprinkle before serving.

Effect: Suitable for the cold season.
Caution: Fresh ginger does not drink over a long period of time.

10 Effects of food

10.1 Use ingredients: recommendable

Barley
Barley not peeled
Beef meat (calf)
Brussels sprouts
Buckwheat (roasted) Kasha
Buckwheat whole grain
Celery sticks
Cherry (sour)
Chicken egg
Chicken yolk
Flower pollen
Kidney beans (red)
Longane
Millet
Millet flakes
Noodles (wheat) with egg
Noodles (whole grain) with egg
Parsley
Pearl barley
Peas, green
Raspberry
Saffron
Savoy cabbage / kale
Sesame, white

10.2 Use ingredients: yes

Acai powder
Acerola fruit nectar or powder
Adzuki beans
Agave nectar
Almond
Almond marzipan
Almond milk
Almond puree
Aloe juice
Amaranth Pops
Angelica root
Apple (sour)
Apple (sweet)
Apple juice (natural cloudy)
Apricot
Apricots
Arrowroot
Artichoke
Baking powder
Balm
Banchatee (green tea)
Barley flour
Barley grouts
Barley malt
Basic recipe for a chicken soup (warming)
Basic recipe for a fish soup
Basic recipe for a rice soup (Congee)
Basic recipe for a vegetable soup (nutritious)
Batavia
Beans (green, fresh)
Beef fillet
Beef kidney
Beef liver
Beef lungs (calf)
Beef meat
Beef meatbones
Beef Oxtail pieces
Beef soup meat
Beef stomach
Beer (Pils)
Beer (Top-fermented German dark beer)
Bitter melon
Black beans
Black fungus mushroom
Blackberry jam
Blackberry´s
Blueberry
Blueberry dried
Blueberry jam
Blueberry juice
Bocksdorn fruits (Fructus Lycii, goji berry dried
Boletus mushroom
Bread roll
Broad beans (thick beans)
Broccoli
Buckwheat
Bush beans
Butter (half fat)
Butter organic
Buttermilk
Calamari
Carp
Carrot
Carrot (Early Carrot)

Carrot juice without sugar
Cashews
Cauliflower
Celery root
Chamomile
Champignon
Chanterelle
Chard
Cherry compote
Chervil
Chervil dried
Chestnuts
Chicken egg white
Chicken liver
Chicken meat
Chicken stomach
Chickpeas
Chicory
Chinese cabbage
Chlorella (fresh water)
Clementines
Coconut flakes
Coconut grated
Coconut milk
Coix (seeds) YiYi Ren
Corn
Corn (fast polenta)
Corn (roasted)
Corn flour
Corn germ oil
Corn Grease (Polenta)
Corn starch
Cow's milk (1.5% fat)
Cow's milk (whole milk 3.5% fat)
Cranberry
Cranberry jam
Cranberry juice
Cream (30% fat)
Cream sour 10%
Cream sour 20%
Cream sour 30%
Cream, sweet 30%
Crème fraiche cheese
Crucian
Curd cheese 20%
Curd cheese 40%
Currant (black)
Currant (red)
Currant (white)
Currants (black)
Currants (red)
Dates dried
Dates red
Deer meat

Duck (heart)
Duck (slaughtered)
Ducks egg
Edam cheese
Eel
Elderberry blossom tee
Emmental cheese
Endive salad
Fennel
Fig
Fig dried
Fish pieces mixed (fresh water)
French beans
Fresh cheese
Fresh cheese from soya
Freshwater fish
Ginger oil
Goat and sheep's liver
Goose
Goose egg
Goose parts
Gooseberry
Gouda cheese
Gourd
Grapes red
Grass carp
Hazelnuts
Herbs different varieties
Herbs various
Herring
Horehound leaves
Horse meat
Iceberg lettuce
Kefir
Kombu seaweed (Saccharina japonica)
Lamb's lettuce
Lemon peel
Lentils red
Lettuce
Licorice root tea
Lima beans
Linseed
Linseed (crushed)
Linseed oil
Loquate / Japanese medlar
Lotus roots
Lotus seeds
Lye roll
Mallow (Malva sylvestris) blossom tea
Malt
Mango juice
Manioc flour
Maple syrup
Mare's milk

Margarine
Margarine (diet)
Morel (black, dried)
Morel, dried
Mozzarella
Multi-grain bread (gray bread)
Mung bean
Nasturtium (nose-twister or nose-tweaker)
Nectarine
Oat
Oat flakes (whole grain)
Oat flour
Oat fusion (baby food)
Oat meal
Octopus
Olive oil
Olives
Oyster mushroom
Oyster shell powder
Oysters
Parmesan
Parsley root
Parsnip
Peanut (roasted)
Peanut butter
Peanut oil
Peanuts
Pear
Pear juice
Pearl barley
Peas
Peppers
Perch
Pigeon
Pine nuts
Pineapple
Pineapple juice without sugar
Pinto beans speckled
Pistachios
Pork ham
Pork ham cooked
Pork heart
Pork knuckle
Pork Lard
Pork skin
Pork stomach
Potato
Potato (mealy)
Potato flour
Processed cheese 12%
processed cheese 30%
Psyllium seed
Pumpernickel (dark bread)

Pumpkin
Pumpkin seed oil
Pumpkin seeds
Quail
Quail egg
Quince
Quinoa
Rabbit
Rabbit meat
Radicchio
Radish black
Radish horseradish
Raisins
Rapeseed oil
Raspberry dried (immature)
Raspberry jam
Red beet
Red berry (without sugar)
Red cabbage
Reishi mushroom
Rice (fragrance)
Rice (Gaoliang / Sorghum)
Rice Basmati
Rice black
Rice long grain rice
Rice mash
Rice noodles
Rice round grain
Rice starch
Rice sticky
Rice sweet
Rice wild (nature rice)
Romaine lettuce / lettuce salad
Rooibos tea
Rusk
Rye
Rye flour
Rye wholemeal bread
Sage
Sago (cereals)
Salmon
Salsify
Salt (herbal)
Sauerkraut (cutted cabbage fermented)
Sea buckthorn
Sesame oil
Sesame oil roasted
Sesame paste (Tahini)
Sesame, black
Shark
Shiitake, dried
Sour cherries
Sour cream (Schmand) 30% fat
Sour cream 15% fat

Sour milk
Soy cream
Soy flour
Soy noodles
Soy Tofu
Soy Tofu smoked
Soya Cuisine (soy cream)
Soybean milk
Soybean oil
Soybeans
Soybeans, black
Soybeans, blacks, fermented
Soybeans, yellow
Spinach
Stevia (candyleaf, sweetleaf)
Strawberry jam
Sugar - icing sugar
Sugar brown
Sugar candy white
Sugar cane sugar
Sugar fructose - fruit sugar
Sugar glucose - grapes sugar
Sugar Milk Sugar
Sugar molasses
Sugar palm sugar
Sunflower oil
Sunflower seeds
Sweet potato
Tangerine
Tarragon (Estragon)
Thistle oil
Tomato dried
Tomato juice
Trout
Truffle
Tsampa (roasted barley flour)

Turnip
Valerian
Vanilla
Vanilla powder
Vegetable juice
Walnuts
Water
Water hot
Wax gourd
Wheat
Wheat bulgur
Wheat flakes
Wheat flatbread/pita bread
Wheat flour
Wheat flour whole grain
Wheat germ oil
Wheat semolina
Wheat semolina for children
Wheat/Rye/Gray-black bread with yeast
Whey
White beans
White bread (baguette)
White bread (pretzel sticks)
White bread (roll)
White bread (wheat bread)
White breadcrumbs
White cabbage
White dumpling bread (wheat bread cut into chunks)
Whole grain bread
Wholemeal bread with whole grains
Wholemeal flour
Yam root, yam root tuber
Yeast
Zucchini

10.3 Use ingredients: little

Anise (Common Fennel)
Apple puree
Apricot dried
Apricot jam
Apricot nectar
Apricots juice
Basic recipe for a duck soup
Basil
Basil (fresh)
Bay leaf
Bean oil
Bearberry leaf
Beef heart
Beef heart (calf)

Beer (alcohol-free)
Beer (alcohol-reduced)
Berries of the season
Berry juice
Bitter liqueur
Black caraway
Blackberry dried (unripe fruit)
Black-eyed peas
Borage oil
Boxhorn clover seeds
Brazil nuts
Breadcrumbs (wheat bread, bread roll)
Brown ale
Bulgur (cereals)

Butter beans white
Cereal coffee
Cherry
Cherry juice
Chicken heart
Chives
Chrysanthemum blossom tea
Clarified butter
Clementine
Clove
Cocoa
Coconut fat
Coconut meat
Codfish
Cola drink
Cola drink (low calorie)
Cooking oil
Coriander (fresh)
Corn silk tea
Cottage cheese
Couscous
Cranberries
Cucumber (spicy cucumber)
Cumin (Caraway seed)
Currant jam (black)
Currant jam (red)
Currant juice (black)
Deer meat
Dill
Dulse (seaweed)
Eel smoked
Elderberries
Fennel seeds ground
Fennel tea
Fernet Branca (herbal bitter liqueur)
Feta cheese
Feta cheese
Fish innards
Fish remains
Fresh cheese with herbs
Gail plum
Gelatin white
Gentian root
Ginger fresh
Ginkgo fruit
Ginseng root
Goat
Goat and sheep's brain
Goat and sheep's milk
Goat and sheep's stomach
Goat cheese
Goose fat
Grapes white
Green spelt

Ground
Ground caraway
Hawthorn
Hokkaido pumpkin
Honey wine (Met)
Hyssop
Juniper berry
Kohlrabi
Kudzu
Kumquats
Lavender blossoms
Leaf salads (bitter)
Leek
Lentils
Lentils black
Lentils yellow
Lovage
Lychee
Lychee in Preserved
Mackerel
Marjoram
Martini
Mascarpone cheese
Mediterranean fish (cod, plaice,
haddock, sea eel, mackerel)
Mirabelle plum
Mustard medium hot
Nettles
Oat flakes roasted
Oat milk
Okra
Olives green
Onion (shallot)
Onion (spring onion)
Onion read
Onion white
Orange jam
Palm oil
Papaya
Peaches
Peaches (canned)
Pepper Cayenne
Pepper powder (hot)
Pepper white (ground)
Peppercorns
Peppermint
Peppermint tea
Peppers (rose peppers)
Peppers powder
Pheasant
Pineapple (from a can)
Pomegranate
Poppy
Pork Bacon

Pork fat (lard)
Pork ham smoked
Pork kidneys
Pork liver
Pork sausage (Bratwurst) Prosecco
Rice (whole grain)
Rice flour
Rice malt
Rice red
Rice variety any
Rose hip
Rose hip tea
Sake
Salt
Savory
Sour milk cheese 20%
Spelled (Dark) bread
Spelled flakes
Spelled grain
Spelled semolina
Spelled wholemeal flour

Star anise
Strawberries
Strawberry Juice
Supplementary nutrition
Thyme
Toast bread (whole grain)
Tomato paste
Tomato puree
Trout (smoked)
Turkey breast meat
Turkey ham
Turmeric (yellow root)
Turnips
Umeboshi paste
Umeboshi plums (Japanese apricots)
Vinegar Aceto Balsamico white
Wakame
White wine
Whitefish
Wild boar meat
Wild garlic (garlic spinach)

10.4 Do not use contra-acting foods

Agar agar (kelp)
Amaranth
Anchovy / Sardine
Asparagus (green or white)
Aubergine
Avocado
Bamboo shoots
Banana
Banana (cooking banana)
Basic recipe for a beef soup (warming)
Beef bone marrow
Bitter Lemon
Black tea
Borage
Brie cheese
Burdock root tea
Camembert
Campari
Cantaloupe
Capers in olive oil
Carambola (Star fruit)
Cardamom
Caviar
Chili (pod or ground)
Chocolate
Cinnamon ground
Cinnamon sticks
Cod
Coffee
Coriander

Crab
Cress
Cucumber
Curry
Curry paste red
Dandelion (young plants)
Dandelionroots tea
Fenugreek (Trigonella foenum-graecum)
Fish sauce
Flounder
Garlic
Ginger powder
Goat and sheep's blood
Goose blood
Gorgonzola
Grape juice red
Grape juice white
Grapefruit (Pomelo)
Grapefruit juice
Green tea
Halibut (Flatfish)
Honey
Hop
Kiwi
Lady's mantle
Lamb bones
Lamb kidneys
Lamb liver
Lamb meat

Lamb shoulder
Lamb's lettuce
Lemon
Lemon Balm (dried)
Lemon Balm (fresh)
Lemon juice
Lime
Lobster
Mango
mango powder
Mineral water
Miso
Miso black (fermented)
Miso paste (soy bean paste)
Mold cheese
Mulberry fruit
Mullet
Mung bean sprouting
Mussels
Mustard
Mustard Dijon
Mustard seeds
Mustard sweet
Mutton
Mutton
Nori, purple seaweed, red algae
Nutmeg
Orange
Orange juice
Oregano dried
Oregano fresh
Pepperoni
Pepperoni, red, pitted, halved
Pepperoni, yellow, pitted, halved
Peppers (sweet)
Pickle
Pimento
Plaice
Plum

Plum dried
Plums
Pork meat
Rabbit (wild)
Rabbit liver
Radish
Radish (white, green, purple-red)
Red wine
Rhubarb
Rosefish
Rosemary
Rum
Seacrab
Sheep's milk
Sheep's milk yoghurt
Shrimp
Shrimps
Sorrel
Soy sauce
Spiny lobsters
Spirit
Spurdog (spiny dogfish, Schillerlocken)
St. Benedict's thistle, blessed thistle, holy thistle, Sugar white
Tabasco
Thyme dried
Tomato
Tuna
Vinegar (Apple vinegar)
Vinegar (Red wine vinegar)
Vinegar Aceto Balsamico
Watermelon
Wheat beer
Wheat bran
Yarrow
Yarrow tea
Yogi tea
Yogurt (natural, 1.5% fat)
Yogurt (natural, 3.5% fat)

11 Complementary

11.1 Adonis vernalis (pheasant's eye, spring pheasant's eye)

Adonis vernalis, herb.
Preparation: Different effects
Calms Heart-Qi, moves Blood, strengthens, diuretic.

11.2 Arnica (wolf's bane)

Arnica montana, flor.
Preparation: Oil for massage
Moves blood, moving heart-blood, moving qi and blood in the upper heater, invigorating qi, tonifies heart-yang.
Arnica blossoms are used in: tissue and organ damage (e.g., mechanical effects and disorders of the blood supply); Injuries such as strains, bruises. After washing, bathing, showering or swimming, massage gently into the still moist skin. During pregnancy use regularly to avoid stretch marks.
Dosage: Prepare massage oil from 10g arnica blossoms and 50g aloe vera oil and leave to stand for 3 weeks (if necessary put in the sun and shake occasionally).
Note: It is not recommended to use arnica internally. It can cause nausea, vomiting and heart problems.

11.3 Chili pods

Capsicum annuum, fruct.
Preparation: Embrocation
Eliminates wind-cold. Warms up inner / Li, moves Heart-Qi and Blood.
Dosage: Note: High doses may lead to life-threatening hypothermia, prolonged use, acute gastritis, inflammation of the kidneys. Capsicum preparations irritate the skin and mucous membranes even in small quantities and may cause painful burning sensations.

11.4 Ginkgo leaves

Ginkgo biloba
Preparation: Decoction
Moves blood. Moves heart blood, strengthens lung-qi, astringent.
Studies prove the effect of Ginko Bilboa concentrate as a highly effective antioxidant, which can protect healthy cells against side effects of the chemotherapy drug adriamycin. Ginko has a tumor-inhibiting effect in cultures of oral and liver cancer cells and protected rats from chemically induced colon cancer in animal experiments.

11.5 Marigold flowers

Calendula officialis, flor.
Preparation: Healing tea (infusion)
Moves moisture, moves liver-qi, strengthens heart-qi, moves blood, diaphoretically.

Active ingredients: Aeth. Oils, calendula-sapogenin, saponins, glycosides, caratonoids, xanthophylls, bitter substances, mucilages, flavonoids, ferments, org. Acids.
Dosage: Tea or gargle water: 1 teaspoon dried herb with 250ml. Water.
Ointment: 2 Handful flowers to 200ml. Heat organic olive oil and 50g beeswax over low heat, strain, fill into jars in portions.
Note: The famous marigold ointment heals rashes, wounds, inflammation and varicose veins. marigoldtea dissolves spasms in abdominal pain and menstrual problems and it promotes bile secretion.

11.6 Sage root

Salvia miltorrhiza, rad.
Preparation: Different effects
Moves and cools heart-blood, calms the heat in the heart and shen, moves blood.
Note: Do not use in pregnancy.

12 Basics of Nutrition

The basic principles of nutrition described herein are general recommendations. They are not aimed at a specific form of therapy. Recommendations concerning a therapy have priority.

12.1 Nutrition

Regular meals in a relaxed atmosphere. A warm breakfast is considered a good start into the day.
The main meals ought to be taken for lunch – supper in the early evening. Pay attention to feeling hungry or sated: don't eat too much nor remain hungry is the rule
Prepare the meals freshly from natural, regional products. Frozen, heat-conserved, industrially prepared or foodstuffs cooked in the microwave oven are rejected.
Choice of foodstuffs according to the season: more cooling food in summer, more warming food in winter.
Eat cooked food at least twice a day. Food and drinks ought to be lukewarm, never ice-cold or hot.
Raw vegetables, briefly cooked vegetables, freshly squeezed juices and mineral water are not recommended. Milk and dairy products are only included in the diet if they don't cause problems.
Don't use therapeutic recipes over a longer period without consulting your doctor or therapist.

Varied food
Enjoy the diversity of foodstuffs. Characteristics of a balanced nutrition are variety, suitable combination and a balanced quantity of rich and low energy foodstuffs (on one hand avoiding undersupply with essential nutrients and on the other hand to take to many undesirable substances).

A lot of Cereal Products - and Potatoes
Bread, pasta, rice, cereal flakes (best wholemeal) as well as potatoes contain almost no fat, but many vitamins, mineral nutrients, trace elements, roughage and secondary plant substances. These foodstuffs ought to be taken with low-fat side dishes.

Vegetables and Fruit – „Take Five" every day ...
5 portions of vegetables and fruit a day, as fresh as possible, briefly cooked, or maybe one portion as a juice – ideal as a side dish to every meal as well as snack between meals: Thus a lot of vitamins, mineral nutrients as well as roughage and secondary plant substances

Daily milk and dairy products
Milk and Dairy Products every Day, once or twice per Week Fish; meat, sausages as well as eggs moderately. These foodstuffs contain valuable nutrients like calcium in the milk, iodine selenium and omega-3 fat acids in saltwater fish. Meat is favorable due to its high content of disposable iron and the vitamins B1, B6 and B12. Quantities of 300 – 600 g meat and sausage per week are sufficient. Prefer low-fat products, especially in meat- and dairy products.

Low-fat and fatty Foodstuffs
Fat supplies us with essential fat acids and fatty foodstuffs contain also fat-soluble vitamins. Fat is high in energy; therefore much fat in the food may cause overweight, possibly also cancer. Too many saturated fat acids may further a tendency for cardio-vascular diseases in the long term. Prefer vegetable oils and fats (e.g. rapeseed-, olive-, soya-oils and solid fats produced therefrom). Beware of invisible fat in meat- and dairy products, pastry and sweets as well as in fast-food and convenience foods. 70 – 90 g fat per day is sufficient.

Moderately Sugar and Salt
Take sugar and foods/drinks containing various kinds of sugar (e.g. glucose syrup) only occasionally. Use herbs and spices as well as a little salt creatively. Prefer salt containing iodine.

Plenty of Liquids
Water is absolutely essential. Drink 1-2 l liquids every day. Prefer water (with or without gas) and other low-calorie drinks. Alcoholic drinks should not be taken.

Tasty Dishes, carefully cooked
Cook the meals with as low temperatures and as short as possible, using little water and fat – this preserves the original taste, keeps the nutrients intact and prevents the production of harmful compounds.

Take time and enjoy the food
Take your Time and enjoy your Food
Eating consciously helps to eat right. The eye enjoys food, too. It's fun, invites to enjoy varied dishes and stimulates the feeling of satiety.

Watch your Weight and stay in Motion
A balanced diet and a lot of exercise and sport (30 – 60 min/day) are a healthy combination. The right weight furthers well-being and health. Thermals, directional effectiveness, digestive power

There are various criteria for judging the effectiveness of herbs and foodstuffs.

The use of certain herbs and ingredients is based on observations of the effects on the body which these foodstuffs, herbs and spices show after having eaten them. The medical science has developed following system: Every ingredient or herb has a directional effectiveness. Furthermore, there are herbs which have a special effect on certain organs.

The basic condition for a healthy metabolism is to obtain sufficient energy from food and that the digestive process doesn't use too much energy. An easily digestible meal makes content and sated, doesn't cause flatulence and fatigue after the meal. The perfect spices increase the healthiness of our meals. Very often, just small doses of herbs and spices will suffice. They are not used to make us sated, but to help our digestive organs to digest the food.

12.2 Recipes

The recipes list the ingredients to be used and the cooking instructions show how the dish is prepared. The list of ingredients shows the concerned quantities as well as the relevance for the therapy. If you find „less than mentioned", try to comply or find an alternative from the „list of recommended foodstuffs". Mostly it shall result just in a small change of taste when you simply avoid this ingredient.

Mild cooking methods: boiling, stewing, poaching, steaming
Strong cooking methods: barbecuing, roasting, frying, smoking
Balanced cooking methods: deep-frying, baking brick
Deep-freezing and warming in the microwave oven should be avoided (denaturalization).

12.3 Foodstuffs

Foodstuffs have an effect on body and soul like medicinal herbs, only a very much milder one. Dietary advice is mainly based on regional foodstuffs. The knowledge about the effects of each foodstuff and the knowledge, when which foodstuff shall be used, is based on the orthodox school of medicine. Use ecologic-organic products, if possible. As everything should be cooked for a long time due to a better digestability and very rarely eaten raw, the food agrees with everyone.

The classification of the foodstuffs according to their effect on the body is the basis in order to achieve a harmonious status of health.

Dietary advisors do not recommend certain foodstuffs for everyone. The individual diet is tailor-made for the individual constitution.

Buy only fresh and ripe fruit and vegetables. You ought to leave unripe fruit and vegetables and such with brown spots and wilted leaves behind in the market. In this case take deep-frozen goods (never ready-to-serve dishes!). Fruit and vegetables are deep-frozen immediately after harvesting and often contain more vitamins and minerals than the goods from the vegetable shelf. Whereas conserved or tinned goods contain very much less biological substances. Also, salt, sugar and others are mostly added to the latter. Never leave the foodstuffs in the water after washing them to avoid that many vital substances get drowned. Clean salads, fruit and vegetables immediately before serving.

Please make sure of the hygienic processing of foodstuffs. Clean your salads, fruit and vegetables carefully. When cooking with meat, prepare all ingredients first and then process the meat products. Clean the worktop and tools very carefully. Wooden surfaces ought to be treated with a mild disinfectant regularly in order to reduce germination.

Store fruit and vegetables separately, if possible. Harvested fruit and vegetables are still alive and emit e.g. ethylene gas, which makes other products ripen and age faster. Keep meat and fish in the closed packaging or store them in the fridge in closed containers.

12.4 Herbs

There are some basic rules for storing medicinal herbs. On principle, herbs must be protected from direct sunlight, humidity and heat.

Containers for the storage of herbs may be glasses, ceramic jars and even plastic containers. However, plastic is a rather unsuitable material and should only be a short-term solution. In case of glass containers, use a dark material.

Medicinal herbs cannot be kept for any long period. The shelf life of herbs is limited. However, it can be prolonged with suitable storage. The place should be dark, rather cool and absolutely dry. A wooden medicine cabinet, placed not directly next to a source of heat, would be ideal. Never buy large quantities of herbs so as not to have to throw them away. Label the container with the name of the herb and the date of harvesting or processing.

13 Other dietic-books

The following syndromes of dietetics, TCM or for a therapy supplement for cancer are available.

Dietetics

E001. Nutrition of the infant - baby food
E002. Nutrition during lactation
E003. Nutrition in old age
E004. Nutrition of children and adolescents
E005. Nutrition of athletes
E006. Light weight
E007. Pregnancy
E008. Full food

Protein and electrolyte - kidneys
E009. (hemodialysis) dialysis treatment
E010. Acute renal failure
E011. Chronic renal insufficiency
E012. Nephrotic syndrome
E013. Kidney stones (nephrolithiasis)

Gastrointestinal tract - pancreas
E014. Acute pancreatitis (inflammation of the pancreas)
E015. Chronic pancreatitis (inflammation of the pancreas)

Gastrointestinal tract - small intestine and large intestine
E016. Acute obstipation (constipation)
E017. Chronic obstipation (constipation)
E018. Colon irritabile
E019. Diverticulitis
E020. Acquired lactose intolerance (lactose malabsorption)
E021. Fructose malabsorption
E022. Glutensensitive enteropathy (celiac disease)
E023. Colectomy
E024. Short Bowel Syndrome

Gastrointestinal tract - liver, gallbladder, bile ducts
E025. Acute and chronic hepatitis (inflammation of the liver)
E026. Cholelithiasis (bile stones)
E027. fatty liver
E028. cirrhosis

Gastrointestinal tract - Stomach and duodenal intestine
E029. Acute gastritis
E030. Chronic gastritis
E031. Stomach bleeding
E032. Ulcus ventriculi and duodenal ulcer
E033. Condition after gastric surgery

Gastrointestinal tract - oral cavity and esophagus
E034. Stomatitis
E035. Esophageal carcinoma (esophageal cancer)
E036. Refluosophagitis (heartburn)

Special diseases
E037. Phenylketonuria (PKU)
E038. Rheumatic joint diseases

Metabolism
E039. Obesity (overweight)
E040. Diabetes mellitus
E041. Eating disorders (underweight)

Fat metabolism
E042. Hypercholesterolaemia (increased cholesterol level)
E043. Hepatic Encephalopathy

Heart and circulation
E044. Arteriosclerosis (arterial calcification)
E045. Heart insufficiency
E046. Hypertension
E047. Hyperuricaemia and gout

Changed nutrient requirements
E048. In case of fever
E049. For malignant diseases
E050. After burns
E051. Radiation and chemotherapy

CANCER
E100. Pancreatic cancer
E101. Bladder cancer
E102. Blood cancer (leukemia)
E103. Breast cancer
E104. Colorectal cancer
E105. Gastric cancer
E106. Kidney cancer
E107. Esophageal cancer

TCM
E200. Bladder - moisture heat in the bladder
E201. Bladder - moisture and cold in the bladder
E202. Bladder - emptiness and cold in the bladder
E203. Large intestine - external cold affects the large intestine
E204. Large intestine - moisture heat in the large intestine
E205. Large intestine - heat blocks the intestine II acute
E206. Large intestine - dryness of the colon
E207. Large intestine - Yang deficiency (cold)
E208. Heart - Blood insufficiency
E209. Heart - Blood stagnation
E210. Heart - Fire
E211. Heart - Hot mucus clogs the heart pores

E212. Heart - Cold mucus clogs the heart pores
E213. Heart - Qi deficiency
E214. Heart - Yang deficiency
E215. Heart - Yin deficiency
E216. Liver - Ascending Liver Yang
E217. Liver - Blood deficiency
E218. Liver - Blood stagnation
E219. Liver - Moisture heat in liver and gall bladder
E220. Liver - Fire
E221. Liver - Gall bladder Qi-Empty
E222. Liver - Cold in the liver meridian
E223. Liver - Qi stagnation
E224. Liver - Wind
E225. Liver - Wind with ascending liver Yang
E226. Liver - Wind with blood anemic
E227. Liver - Wind with extreme heat
E228. Lung - Qi deficiency
E229. Lung - Mucus-moisture in the lungs
E230. Lung - Mucus-heat in the lungs
E231. Lung - Mucus-cold in the lungs
E232. Lung - Dryness of the lungs
E233. Lung - Wind-heat attacks the lungs
E234. Lung - Wind-cold affects the lungs
E235. Lung - Yin deficiency
E236. Stomach - Bloodstagnation
E237. Stomach - Fire
E238. Stomach - Cold with liquid
E239. Stomach - Nutrition stagnation
E240. Stomach - Qi deficiency
E241. Stomach - Rebellious Qi
E242. Stomach - Yin Emptiness
E243. Spleen - Heat and moisture attack the spleen
E244. Spleen - Coldness and moisture affects the spleen
E245. Spleen - Qi deficiency
E246. Spleen - Qi deficiency + Declining spleen Qi
E247. Spleen - Qi deficiency + spleen does not control the blood
E248. Spleen - Yang deficiency
E249. Kidney - Heart and kidney no longer communicate
E250. Kidney - Jing deficiency
E251. Kidney - Kidneys cannot receive the Qi
E252. Kidney - Qi is not stable
E253. Kidney - Yang deficiency
E254. Kidney - Yin deficiency

For further information visit di-book.com.

14 EBNS - Software for nutritional counseling

The main task of the database is to create personalized nutritional advice for each patient individually. The database was developed for Dietetics

and Traditional Chinese Medicine.
The Database supports training and advices in the daily work routine.

The computer program provides lists of recipes, ingredients and herbs, which are given to the client. individually adjustable according to patient's request from whole food to vegetarians (lacto, ovo, ...). For every register there is an information sheet which can be given to the client. All texts can be individually designed.

The syndromes can be combined and result in an intersection of the recommended recipes and ingredients. The automated diagnosis for the TCM enables you to check your experience during the training as well as to confirm your diagnosis in the working day. You select several predefined symptoms and have the program automatically display the relevant syndromes.

How to work with the database:
Select the patient / client, select one or more of the syndromes you diagnosed and print the folder.

You can change all values, create new symptoms or syndromes, develop recipes, change or adapt ingredients and herbs to your findings. In simple client management, all relevant data about the person is stored. You get an overview of the past diagnoses and the development of the course of the disease.

As a consultant you save a lot of time when you print out the recipe, food and herbal lists for the recognized syndromes and give them to the clients. You can use this time for a personal conversation. With the database, dieticians and nutritionists can view the nutrients and trace elements for each recipe and develop recipes for syndromes even with suggested ingredients.

All recipe and grocery lists can also be ordered from me as a combination of several diseases. I wish all readers good luck, health and happiness in life.
More information can be found at www.ebns.at.
Volunteer: www.krebsinfo.at
Josef Miligui